ANGELS
ARE EVERYWHERE

WHAT THEY ARE, WHERE THEY
COME FROM, AND WHAT THEY DO

ANGELS
ARE EVERYWHERE

WHAT THEY ARE, WHERE THEY COME FROM, AND WHAT THEY DO

BY KAREN ROMANO YOUNG

ILLUSTRATED BY
NATHAN HALE

ALADDIN
NEW YORK LONDON TORONTO SYDNEY

For Mom

ALADDIN

An imprint of Simon & Schuster Children's Publishing Division

First Aladdin paperback edition October 2009

1230 Avenue of the Americas, New York, NY 10020

Text copyright © 2009 by Karen Romano Young

Illustrations copyright © 2009 by Nathan Hale

All rights reserved, including the right of reproduction in whole or in part in any form.

ALADDIN is a trademark of Simon & Schuster, Inc., and related logo is a registered trademark of Simon & Schuster, Inc.

For information about special discounts for bulk purchases, please contact Simon & Schuster Special Sales at 1-866-506-1949 or business@simonandschuster.com.

The Simon & Schuster Speakers Bureau can bring authors to your live event. For more information or to book an event contact the Simon & Schuster Speakers Bureau at 1-866-248-3049 or visit our website at www.simonspeakers.com.

Designed by Lisa Vega

The text of this book was set in Adobe Garamond.

Manufactured in the United States of America

10 9 8 7 6 5 4 3 2 1

Library of Congress Control Number 2008943448

ISBN 978-1-4169-6447-6

ISBN 978-1-4169-9768-9 (eBook)

CONTENTS

CHAPTER SIX:

ANGELS IN YOUR LIFE

ANGELS
ARE EVERYWHERE

WHAT THEY ARE, WHERE THEY COME FROM, AND WHAT THEY DO

Do You Believe in Angels?

MOST PEOPLE DO.

H alo there. If you answered YES to the question above, you're not alone. And that's just one reason that this is a tricky book to write.

1. Seventy-five percent of Americans answered YES when asked if they believed in angels, as reported in a 2007 Gallup Poll. An extra 11 percent thought there *might* be angels; they weren't sure. So you have to be really careful what you say about angels.

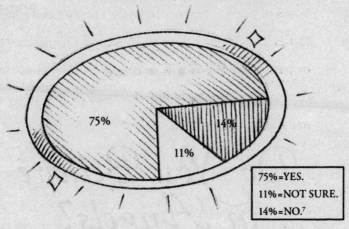

75%

14%

11%

75%=YES.
11%=NOT SURE.
14%=NO.[7]

2. Most people know what angels are and what they do. Many people can name and describe angels. Some people even remember meeting angels. But nobody can summon an angel to stand up, show itself, and say "here I am," and there is no other way to prove the existence of angels. Discussions of things outside physical experience can annoy people or make them shut down. So you have to be really careful what you say.

3. For many people, angels are a matter of faith, something they believe in without having any proof. Discussions of faith and personal spirituality can easily offend people. So you have to be really careful.

4. Angels are part of the stories that form the most holy books of many different religions. They are also part of stories associated with religions but not considered to be part of the holy books. Discussions of religions and their outlook on the world can make people angry or make them debate with you. So you have to be . . .

I have to be honest. I probably can't be careful enough for some people. I don't know what parts of this book are true by

> *But if the archangel now, perilous, from behind the stars took even one step down toward us: our own heart, beating higher and higher, would beat us to death. Who are you?* —Rainer Maria Rilke, *Duino Elegies*: 2

many definitions of the word true. I just know that **angelology**—the study of angels—is one of the most fantastic things I've ever come across. The stories are glorious, the art is heavenly, and the ideas of what angels can be—the link between heaven and Earth, heaven and hell, the living and the dead, humans and God—are truly WONDERFUL. And many, many people of different religions (or no religion at all) believe in angels.

So I'm going to tell you what I've found out. And you're

going to take it with a grain of salt, because usually when something is considered true or possible by 86 percent of Americans, there's all kinds of proof. Well, with angels, there just isn't.

If you'll excuse the expression, I don't want to fly in the face of facts or faith.

This book is about what we think we know about angels, and why we think we know it, and what it means about us that we think it.

It's also about how believing in something beautiful, mysterious, kind, fierce, and loving changes people. And that is my favorite thing about it. All kinds of people now and in the past—and probably in the future, too—have had their lives changed for the better by angels.

You'll find that this book is full of questions. The answers are always what someone says. The only *facts* involve who gave the answer, and where, and when. The different "experts" are historians, theologians, scribes, storytellers, angelologists, and people who claim to have seen or met angels. What's the real answer? That's up to you to decide. Nobody knows for sure, except the angels.

Angel Lore

HOW DO WE KNOW ABOUT ANGELS?

Where do we get our ideas about angels? From stories, and from histories. From books that are sacred (written or dictated by God), possibly sacred, and not sacred.

For a long, long time, people kept track of their histories and stories by word of mouth. These oral traditions (stories told anytime two or more people were together) became part of the books that form the centers of the big four Western religions: Judaism, Zoroastrianism, Christianity, and Islam.

MAJOR MESSAGE: *Each of the holy books of the big four Western religions includes stories in which angels were sent by God to humans. These are the start of people's understanding of what angels do. But it isn't necessarily the start of angels, which may have roots in folklore, traditions, and stories that came before the holy books.*

The holy book stories told of beings that traveled by flying. How would *you* describe something you'd never seen before, without comparing it to something else—a bird, a kite, a plane, a spaceship? Which comparison would be most appropriate? Lots of people who have studied the idea of angels think that their image came not just from the holy books, but from stories that were told in different cultures.

The *scriptures* are works believed to definitely have been written by God (through an angel), or by writers who were directed by God. (This kind of writer is called a prophet.) Some other books were written by people who might have been angels or prophets, or might not. These books are called *apocrypha*. One of the most famous apocryphal writers, Enoch, wrote at about the same time that the early Bible was written. He describes his dramatic and glorious visit to the center of heaven, where God is found. Enoch's stories aren't scripture, so many people argue about whether they were true. Along with other apocrypha, Enoch's writings have been used by people researching angels all through history, even if the rabbis, priests, and imams said they are not God's word.

THE JEWISH ANGELS

Angels are mentioned 103 times in the Tanakh, the Bible of the Jews, which includes the five books of Moses (the Torah), the books of the Prophets (Nevi'im), and the writings (Kethuvim), including the psalms. Powerful, physical, and fierce angels appear to do God's will. They strike down armies, visit with humans, even challenge a man to a

> ### ANGELIC IDEA
>
> In a room full of people, talk suddenly halts. To fill the awkward moment, somebody might say, "An angel is walking through the room."

wrestling match. Angels talk with Yahweh's (God's) prophets, including David, Elias, Daniel, and Zacharias.

Today, Jews believe in angels as guardians, messengers, and intermediaries, beings with the ability to take people's concerns and prayers to God.

There are now close to fourteen million Jews in the world.[2]

The other three major religions are also based on one supreme being—Ahura Mazda, God, or Allah. Stories in

THE FOUR MAJOR WESTERN RELIGIONS

RELIGION	LEADER	SUPREME BEING
Judaism	Abraham	Yahweh
Zoroastrianism	Zarathustra	Ahura Mazda
Christianity	Jesus	God (Jesus is God's son)
Islam	Muhammed	Allah

their holy books—the Avesta, the Bible, the Qu'ran—show God acting to create the world, to send the great flood, to send laws, to send angels.

THE ZOROASTRIAN ANGELS

Zoroaster, or Zarathustra, lived between 1000 and 600 B.C. in Bactria (in the area of what is now northern Afghanistan). Before Zoroaster, people worshiped many different beings, such as gods and goddesses, who ruled the sun, the moon, music, health, and so on. But Zoroaster changed the pattern of religion in his part of the world: He said there was only one God.

In Zoroastrianism, the one god, the "wise Lord," is

	HOLY BOOK	START OF RELIGION	BELIEVERS
	Tanakh (Bible Old Testament)	2000 to 1500 B.C.	Jews
	Avesta	Around 600 to 1000 B.C. (no definite dates)	Zoroastrians
	Bible New Testament	30 A.D.	Christians
	Qu'ran	622 A.D.	Muslims

Ahura Mazda. But Ahura Mazda has help: angels. Early Zoroastrian stories of the seven archangels closely followed those told of the old Babylonian and Assyrian gods, and Judaic and Christian stories adapted bits of these stories into their own traditions.

There are now about three million Zoroastrians in the world.

NAMES FOR ANGELS

sons of God	the heavenly host
ministers	the heavenly army
ministering spirits	hosts
servants	living creatures
watchers	spirits
the holy ones	the court of heaven

THE CHRISTIAN ANGELS

Besides the many angel stories in the Old Testament of the Bible, Christians follow the teachings of the New

Testament, in which angels are mentioned on nearly every page. Jesus spoke of them fifteen times, telling about their activities and their lives in heaven.

Angels were with Jesus to guide, guard, and encourage him when he was being tempted by Satan in the desert. Angels announced Jesus's birth, helped him face Satan, and announced his resurrection. They even rolled the stone away from his tomb so he could get out.

The Book of Revelation, the last book in the New Testament of the Christian Bible, has thundering, vivid scenes in which angels do battle against Satan's forces.

There are now more than two billion Christians in the world.

ANGELS IN YOUR LIFE

Here's an idea: Just for one day, keep your eyes open for angels. You'll be surprised how often they come up in conversation ("She's his guardian angel." "He's a perfect angel."), in stores (everything from angel food cake to lapel-pin angels and magnets that say "Teachers Are Angels"), in music (one expert says that one in ten pop songs mentions angels), on clothes, stationery, stained-glass windows, TV commercials, and much, much more.

Each time you come across an angel, ask yourself what the angel represents in this situation: Protection? Perfection? Kindness? Love? Self-sacrifice?

THE ISLAMIC ANGELS

The Qu'ran, the Muslim holy book, is believed to have been dictated to the prophet Muhammed by the angel Gabriel. Belief in angels is one of the Islamic Articles of Faith; belief in God's messengers is another.

Muslims believe that two angels accompany each person through life. They guide the person, guard him, and keep records of every good and bad thing he does. At the end of life, the angel of death comes to escort the person out of this life. Although none of these angels is visible, their presence can be clearly felt at times through *wahy*, a moment when angels communicate by placing a message directly into a person's mind.

There are now about 1.5 billion Muslims in the world.

All the holy book stories add up to create our western view of what angels are—God's warriors and messengers—and what they mean to us. They are our link to God, bringing out what is best in us and showing us how deeply we are treasured and loved.

NONRELIGIOUS ANGELS

Angels seem to go beyond just one culture, one religion, one role, or one idea.

There are many other religions, of course, and many Western people are devoted to non-Western religions. But the third largest religious "group" in the world (after Christians and Muslims) are described as nonreligious people. They include:

- atheists, people who don't believe in God.
- agnostics, people who don't believe in any particular religion.
- people who believe in the human spirit.
- people who believe in the spirit of the natural universe.

There are more than one billion nonreligious people in the world. Many of them believe in angels of different sorts.

Some other key thinkers

HE SAW AN ANGEL

First century
A "man of Macedonia" appeared to St. Paul at Troas during the night and asked him to come to Macedonia—on the other side of the sea—to help the Macedonians. Many people think the vision was an angel.

and theologians have added to our "picture" of angels too. They include scholars of the Jewish, Christian, and Muslim faiths. And they include artists and writers who have provided more and more images of angels up through the Middle Ages. Along with the writers of scripture and apocryphal stories, here are some of the people who have made important additions and subtractions to angel lore:

Enoch. Begun in the second century B.C., these are the stories of the prophet Enoch's journey into heaven. Some say that Enoch was taken to heaven by God, who turned him into the angel Metatron.

Pseudo-Dionysius wrote *De Hierarchia Celestia* in about 500 A.D. This book influenced Christian thinking about the hierarchy and powers of angels. One key idea was that people communicate best with God after their bodies die and their spirits go to meet God.

Council of 745. Pope Zachary and his council went through the angel stories and tossed out all angels that weren't specifically mentioned in the Bible. Only Raphael, Gabriel, and Michael remained.

St. Thomas Aquinas. In 1259 he lectured about angels at the University of Paris, basing what he said on scripture, apocrypha, and his own understanding of the world. (Unlike other people who wrote about angels, Aquinas never claimed to have seen an angel.)

Death of Faith. Beginning in the 1340s, the Great Plague killed most of the population of Europe. People lost faith in the angels, and in God Himself. The Church responded by trying to figure out who was to

THEY SAW AN ANGEL

Twenty-first century
Michelle McKenzie, who owns a shop called The Littlest Angel in Connecticut, attended an angel communication workshop, where she envisioned her personal angel—a teenage girl—and learned her name. Later, a minister who specializes in clairvoyance (seeing beyond the physical world), told her that he "saw" an angel near her: a teenage girl with the name Michelle had been given. Michelle credits her angel for pushing her to buy her store and to reach out to her customers with kindness, understanding, and information about how they can get in touch with their angels.

ST. THOMAS AQUINAS

blame. In a period called the Inquisition, suspects were called into church courts and examined carefully for signs that they had been taken over by the devil. Those who seemed "possessed" were condemned to death.

Birth of Science. Then came a period of new learning about the universe. At first men of science were condemned, along with their findings. One famous example was Galileo Galilei, the astronomer who reported that Earth revolved around the sun. So the sun was the center of the universe, not Earth.

John Calvin (1509–1564) rejected the teaching of St. Thomas Aquinas. He agreed that angels carry out God's work and show people God's brilliance. But he thought that if God wanted people to know more about angels,

A MOST IMPORTANT ANGEL

Michael:
- has a name that is a question. According to the Talmud, it means "Who is like God?"
- is said to be the first angel to bow to Adam at God's command, after Lucifer—the angel nearest to God—refused to bow to Adam and was thrown out of heaven. Now Michael is the most important angel of all.
- is believed by Jehovah's Witnesses to be Christ.[8]
- is called Mikha'il in the Qu'ran, where he is said to be second to Gabriel. Mikha'il has saffron hair that grows all the way to his feet, and wings like green topaz. He speaks a million languages. He never laughs.
- was sent with Gabriel by God to find clay so that God could make Adam.

• • • • • • • • • • • • • •CONTINUED ON NEXT PAGE • • • • • • • • • • • • • • •

is often seen in Christian art dressed in armor and a helmet, carrying a shield and a sword or lance.

- is the guardian angel of Israel. When the fallen angel Samael attacked Michael, pulling him down by his wings, Michael fought back. This story came to be told as St. Michael fighting a dragon.

- will one day lead an army of angels against Satan, according to John in the Book of Revelation. The war cry of the angels is Michael's name.

- will weigh souls on Judgment Day, so he carries a scale.

- is the hero of hundreds of stories told and retold down the years. In England the story of Michael and the dragon was retold with St. George as the hero, replacing the archangel. But Michael himself replaced Greek and Roman gods, so that hilltop temples to the gods Hermes and Mercury were rededicated as chapels to Michael. In Germany, Christians replaced the pagan god Wotan, master of the mountaintops, with St. Michael. St. Michael's mounts—hilltop chapels—are found in many parts of Europe.

- is celebrated on Michaelmas, September 29.

- is the angel of healing.

- is the patron saint of police officers, sailors, soldiers, and paratroopers.[9]

there would be more in scripture about them.

Emanuel Swedenborg (1688–1772), a 1700s Swedish chemist, bishop, and theology professor (teacher of religious studies), learned Hebrew so he could study the earliest holy book stories of angels. He said that he had been visited by angels and attacked by devils. He was considered an authority on angels.

Rudolf Steiner (1861–1925) pioneered the Waldorf School system, which aims to feed a child's soul, body, and spirit.

ANGELIC?

In Tibetan Buddhism *devas* is the name for the "emanations" of enlightened beings—the physical manifestations of these spirits who otherwise cannot be seen by people.

He believed in reincarnation—the theory that people's souls pass through different bodies—and that the souls are guided by an angel that stays with them through all the incarnations. Steiner said that people were most aware of their angels in childhood and in old age.

BRANCHES AND WINGS

Very little was added to angel lore for hundreds of years, up to the twentieth century, when people stopped telling stories about the heavens, and actually began to go there in spaceships.

BOOK ANGEL

In *Skellig* by David Almond, Michael finds a winged, man-size creature, injured and starving in a garage.

The Space Age made angel

stories come alive again, as people wondered whether even the oldest stories—Ezekiel's encounter with multi-eyed seraphim, Enoch's tales of brilliant cherubim and the whirling wheels of angels called "thrones"—were really descriptions of extraterrestrials who came to Earth from other planets.

Like angels, aliens seemed to know all about us. They were kind to us. They brought us messages, and blinded us with their strange light. People wanted to know more.

The new knowledge came with the New Age, a twenty-first-century movement that found many people trying to get in touch with their own personal angels. Now adults

[Skellig Michael is] an incredible, impossible, mad place. I tell you the thing does not belong to any world that you and I have lived and worked in; it is part of our dream world.
—George Bernard Shaw

were taking special classes, clicking on websites, and reading books to learn how to call on their angels for guidance, companionship, and inspiration.

- A *stele* (a memorial made of stone) found in the city of Ur, 4000–1500 B.C., shows a winged figure descending from one of seven heavens. This is considered the earliest representation of an angel.

- Assyrian palaces were guarded by *karibu*, similar to the angels called cherubim. They had the heads of men, bodies of lions or bulls, and wings.

- An Etruscan tomb featured a painting of a demon, 500 B.C.

- *The Kairos of Trogir*, 300 B.C., was a winged god that looked like the angels envisioned by Christian artists one thousand years later.

- Early angels were made to look like Greek goddesses, particularly Nike, who flew. This famous statue from 190 B.C., called *Winged Victory*, shows Nike.

- The oldest known Christian image of an angel was painted in A.D. 64 or later on the walls of the catacombs, where Christians hid from those who would kill them. Note: There are no wings or halos on the angels, but each saint's image has a *nimbus*, an aura of light that glows around him or her.

- Christian angels were not shown with wings until nearly A.D. 400. By then, they had wings, halos, and an aura of light.

- In 787 the second council of Nicaea made it lawful to show angels in art. When artists looked around for ideas about how to depict angels, they found inspiration in the Greek gods, especially Nike, the Winged Victory, and Eros, or Cupid.

- During the Middle Ages, Christian artists modeled the wings of angels on those of powerful birds.

Their wings became larger and
more effective-looking.

Is This an Angel?

The Blue Angels flight precision team (part of the U.S. Navy) is one example of the idea that angels exist on a different plane from mere mortals. Not only are they immortal, but they don't have to worry about the laws of physics, including gravity, time, and space.

Where to Find Angels

WHO'S WHO IN HEAVEN, EARTH, AND HELL?

O ur understanding of angels comes from stories. Many of these stories are found in the holy books of the major religions, such as the book of the prophet Ezekiel in the Bible. They are considered holy because they are believed to have been directly written or inspired by God. There are other stories too, such as those told by Enoch, which contain some of the same ideas and events as the holy stories. Were they

HE SAW ANGELS

Sixth century
Mohammed told of going to heaven and seeing an angel with seventy thousand heads. Each head had seventy thousand faces, and each face had seventy thousand mouths. Each mouth had seventy thousand tongues speaking seventy thousand languages.
People of most faiths agree that the angels are without number, there are so many of them. The Jewish Kabbalah—Jewish mystical lore—is precise about the number of angels: 49 MILLION.

just "stories"? Or were they histories? Because religious experts through the ages have been unsure of the answer, the apochryphal stories have been set aside. They're not *in* the holy books, but you might say they're on a shelf nearby.

Both Enoch and Ezekiel describe extended tours to the heart of heaven and back. They say that the Almighty God is at the center of the universe. God is surrounded by angels that praise him, do his work, carry his messages, and even go to battle for him.

The Bible begins with creation. In the Book of Genesis, God creates the world as a Paradise. He makes Adam and Eve and gives them the job of naming all living things. But when Adam and Eve disobey God and are cast out of Paradise, the apochryphal story follows them. Paradise—

a place where mortal man can live with immortal God—is left behind.

Now the heavens are walled off from humans. Sin and death is something humans experience here in our world, but it doesn't exist in heaven. The border between heaven and Earth is guarded by the angels. But which angels?

When we use the word *angels*, we are usually talking about ones who are nearest to humans and who have the most interaction with people, watching over us closely and giving us messages. These are actually the angels of the ninth choir. There are eight other heavenly choirs, each with its own kind of angels: seraphim, cherubim, ophanim, dominions, virtues, powers, principalities, and archangels.

So the angels nearest Earth are actually the lowest of the

Is This an Angel?

Cupid shows up on Valentine's Day to shoot his arrow at lovers to make them find each other more appealing. He has wings, and nowadays he looks like a cherub—that is, a *putti*, a fat baby angel. In the past, Cupid looked more like an angel—usually a young, male one. But Cupid has his roots in mythology. He is modeled on the Greek god Eros (or the Roman god Amor), who was the god of love.

angels. Like all angels, they are without sin. They are tempted by being human, but if they sin, they can no longer be angels. They fall from God's grace.

Why would angels want to be human? Hundreds of stories have been told about such situations, but basically it comes down to this: If angels watch over us and come to love us, then they might want to be closer to us. They may become torn between what God wants and what they want for us. And angels must choose God's way in order to remain holy—or descend to a hell with as many depths as heaven has heights.

Mortals can't see this invisible, nonphysical universe of heaven and hell, but people have imagined it anyway, creating drawings, diagrams, maps, and models. The pictures of the levels of heaven and hell are different: They might show disks, domes, roots, or branches. What they all have in common is angels.

Imagine heaven as a nest of skies, one vaulting over the next. There are seven heavens in all. Seventh heaven—where God is found—is the highest. The first heaven lies next to our own world; it's the Garden of Eden, where Adam and Eve lived before they sinned and were evicted.

Where does this idea of seven heavens come from? It's found in the Kabbalah—the mystical teachings of Judaism, and also in the Qu'ran. It's part of the traditions of ancient Babylonia (where the Jews were held captive) and Persia, the center of Zoroastrianism.

HE SAW AN ANGEL

Eighteenth century
Did a dark, shadowy angel show George Washington a vision of the United States, with towns and cities extending "from sea to shining sea"? Ever since the harsh winter of 1777 at Valley Forge, historians have debated whether the father of our country really had such an experience.

Want a career working with angels? Kermie Wohlenhaus, founder of the School of Angel Studies in Portland, Oregon, an angelologist, is also a *clairvoyant*, someone gifted at seeing beyond the physical world. Her school offers training to become a Certified Intuitive Angel Consultant. She teaches courses on connecting with your guardian angel, finance angel, and love angel. After she speaks, audience members often come to her to talk about their experiences with angels. She says, "Angels are real."

The angels in each heaven have distinct positions and jobs. Some say there are seven levels of Earth, too, hooked carefully one by one onto the edges of the domes of the heavens. Below all is the abyss of hell, an endless pit.

WHO'S WHO IN HEAVEN

God is said to be at the golden core of the universe, a force of light and energy so strong that only the most powerful angels can be near it.

These are the first order—cherubim, seraphim, and thrones—which praise God continually and transform His energy down to the lower orders toward Earth. In Islam, these angels have seventy thousand heads, each with seventy thousand mouths that speak seventy thousand languages—

all used to praise God. They do not have a specific name, as the angels of this order do in Judaism and Christianity.

THE FIRST ORDER OF THE HEAVENS

1. Cherubim: Endless Praise

Job: The main job of the cherubim is to guard the gates of Eden, to stop Adam and Eve—and all sinful men—from coming back. They rule over the stars. The cherubim carry the throne on which God sits. They never stop praising God, using words such as "Holy, holy, holy, Lord God Almighty, who was and is to come!" This sounds boring—but in heaven there is no past and future, only the present, because only humans live in a world governed by time and space.

Looks: Ezekiel described the cherubim as having four faces and four wings.

Name: The word *cherub* comes from *karibu,* "a communicator" in the ancient language of Assyria. These are the winged beings that guarded the Assyrian palaces (see page 21).

Most famous cherubim: Cherubim guard the Ark of the

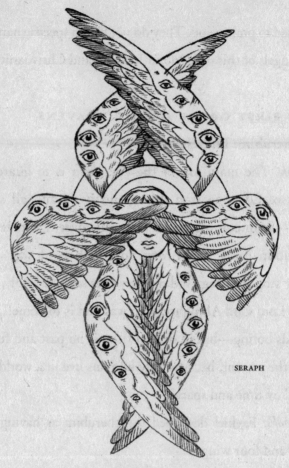

SERAPH

Covenant, the holy chest that holds the Ten Commandments.

More: The Qu'ran says that the cherubim are among the nearest to Allah. They are formed of the tears of the archangel Michael, who cries about people's sins.

Note: Nowadays, *putti*—babyish, chubby angels—are often referred to as cherubs.

2. Seraphim: Hunk O' Burning Love

Job: The main job of the seraphim is to love God, to send out God's love to the universe, and to inspire people to burn with love for God. Like the cherubim, they never stop praising God, chanting or singing "Holy, holy, holy" without end.

Looks: The prophet Isaiah, who lived about 740 B.C., described the seraphim as having six wings: two to fly, two to cover their faces, and two to cover their feet.

Name: The word *seraphim*—"burning one"—comes from the Hebrew word *saraf,* which means to destroy with fire. Without burning himself, one seraph picked up a live coal and used it to cleanse Isaiah's lips so that he could speak to God.

Most famous seraph: Raphael.

More: Enoch said that the seraphim burn the books of Satan, in which he keeps lists of the sins of Israel.

3. Ophanim or Thrones: Where God Rests

Job: Thrones are the chariots of God, with a seat and wheels. The cherubim drive them. They rule over the laws of nature and of justice.

Location: The fourth heaven.

Looks: Thrones have many eyes, and enormous wheels that can go in every direction at once.

Name: Thrones are sometimes called ophanim, chariots, or wheels.

> As I looked at the living creatures, I saw a wheel on the ground beside each creature with its four faces. This was the appearance and structure of the wheels: They sparkled like chrysolite, and all four looked alike. Each appeared to be made like a wheel intersecting a wheel. As they moved, they would go in any one of the four directions the creature faced; the wheels did not turn about as the creatures went. Their rims were high and awesome, and all four rims were full of eyes all around.
>
> —The Bible: Ezekiel, 1:15–18

More: Catholics say the Virgin Mary sits at the throne of God, surrounded by *putti*, the baby angels.

Note: Thrones are not spirit-beings, as the rest of the angels are.

4. Dominions: Angel Authorities

Job: Dominions are in charge of all the angels and their work.

Looks: In the Testament of Adam, dominions ride into battle on red horses.

Name: Dominations or lords.

5. Virtues: On the Edge

Job: Virtues represent the first edge of the border between heaven and Earth. Because they are closer to heaven than to

---

A MOST IMPORTANT ANGEL

Uriel:

- is the archangel of salvation. He is said to be the archangel who warned Noah of the flood.
- is the angel of music.
- is said to be one of the four angels of the Presence, meaning that he sees God's face.
- is both a seraphim and a cherubim.
- rules over hell from heaven.
- is considered the strongest angel besides Metatron, and may have been the one who wrestled Jacob.
- rules the month of September.

Earth, they make miracles happen. Miracles are defined as things that shouldn't happen according to the normal laws of Earthly physics. Water turns to wine, someone comes back from the dead, a guardrail appears where there was only a chasm. Virtues are the highest of the angels who reach out to humans, helping them find calm and courage in frightening times. They are commanded by the dominions.

Looks: Virtues are described as the "shining ones."

Most famous virtues: Legend says two virtues helped Eve as she gave birth to her first son, Cain.

6. POWERS: DOWN WITH DARKNESS

Job: Powers rule over demons, the spirits of darkness in league with Satan, to keep them from taking over the world.

Most famous powers: Samael and Camael, dark angels,

are each described as the leader of the powers, depending on who tells the story.

THE THIRD ORDER OF THE HEAVENS

The third order is often shown in art dressed as soldiers. Note that the art is usually Christian art, and that these angels will go to battle to fight for the souls of humans. Whom are they fighting? The forces of darkness, led by Satan.

One idea of guardian angels is that a pair of good and bad angels is assigned to each individual person. Even though all of us battle evil within ourselves, many find it reassuring to think the warrior angels are fighting a continual battle with Satan's soldiers in the realms outside Earth.

BOOK ANGEL

A Wind in the Door, by Madeleine L'Engle, the sequel to *A Wrinkle in Time*, features Proginoskes, at first mistaken for a "drive" of dragons because he is so full of wings and eyes. Proginoskes insists on being called "cherubim," feeling himself to be more plural than singular. He becomes Meg Murry's friend and guide as she tries to save the life of her brother by traveling through his body at the cell level. The book echoes the world-within-a-world theme of the descriptions of the heavens.

7. PRINCIPALITIES: THE GOD SQUAD

Job: Principalities protect people who pray, do good, praise God, and in other ways try to be closer to God. They rule religion. They may be assigned to watch over specific nations and cities.

8. ARCHANGELS: THE A TEAM

Job: Archangels rule over the physical world, including people and animals.

Looks: Archangels in Islam have thousands of wings.

Name: Archangel means "chief messenger." In the Christian Bible, the word *archangel* appears only in two places, both in the New Testament. It does not appear at all in the Old Testament.

> ### ANGELIC?
>
> Hindu helpful spirits include messenger spirits that are devas and *apsaras*—beautiful fairies or angels of heaven.

Most famous archangels: Ahura Mazda, the Zoroastrian God, relies on six archangels or "divine sparks"—the *amesha spenta*—each with its own realm: Manah governs Purpose, Asha rules Righteousness, Kshathra rules Dominion, Armaiti governs Devotion,

Haurvatat rules Wholeness and Health, and Ameretat rules Immortality.

Seven important angels are also mentioned in the New Testament, in the Book of

> *Praise be to Allah, Who created (out of nothing) the heavens and the earth. Who made the angels, messengers with wings—two, or three, or four (pairs): He adds to Creation as He pleases: for Allah has power over all things.*
> —The Qu'ran, 35:1

Revelation (8:2–5). These angels stand before the throne of God.

In Islam, the archangels are Jibrail (Gabriel), Mikail (Michael), Israfil (Raphael), and Izra'il (Azrael).

In the Book of Revelation, in the Christian New Testament, four archangels rule the points of the compass: Michael (east); Raphael (west); Gabriel (north); Uriel (south).

> *It is not known precisely where angels dwell—whether in the air, the void, or the planets. It has not been God's pleasure that we should be informed of their abode.*
> —Voltaire

9. ANGELS: THE HEAVENLY HOST

Job: The angels are God's workers on Earth. They carry messages, and help and guard people and animals.

Name: The word *angel* comes from the Greek word

aggelos. This is a translation of the word *malak—messenger* in the languages of the Qu'ran (Arabic) and Bible (Hebrew).

ANGELS VERSUS ETS

Stories of angels have been around since the beginning of recorded history, but stories of extraterrestrials have only been told since the 1940s, when a pilot reported seeing a chain of unidentified flying objects over Washington State. The U.S. Air Force began an investigation—and the public began reporting more and more sightings. Some of these

HOW MANY ANGELS ARE THERE?

The Hebrew word *sabaoth* is used to describe the angels as a group. It means a host—many, many angels. Just how many? There are many different answers, some more specific than others.
Here are a few:
- According to medieval Jewish scholars, there are 301,655,722 angels.[3] The Kabbalah puts the number at forty-nine million.
- *Thousands of thousands ministered to Him, and ten thousand times a hundred thousand stood before Him.* —The Bible: Daniel 7: 9–10
- *Do you think I cannot call on my Father, and he will at once put at my disposal more than twelve legions* of angels?* —Jesus, the Bible: Matthew 26:53

*A legion may be between one thousand and five thousand.

 40

reports involved more than just a glimpse of extra-terrestrial beings.

People say they were invited aboard spaceships, shown unknown worlds, and sent home again changed. They describe the ETs in the way angels are sometimes described—as kindly, peaceable guardians

> *Heaven, too, was very near to them in those days. God's direct agency was to be seen in the thunder and the rainbow, the whirlwind and the lightning. To the believer, clouds of angels and confessors, and martyrs, armies of the sainted and the saved, were ever stooping over their struggling brethren upon earth, raising, encouraging, and supporting them.*
> —Sir Arthur Conan Doyle,
> *The White Company*

with special understanding of the universe who watched over Earth and chose these "guests" specially in order to give them a message.

J. Allen Hynek, chairman of Northwestern University's Department of Astronomy, ran the UFO project that began in the 1940s and came up with three degrees of close encounters with aliens: sighting (the first kind), evidence (the second kind), and contact (the third kind). Like angels, UFOs come flying down in a bright flood of light. Is it possible that the stories many people have told over the centuries about meeting angels were actually close

RANK	MANAGERS OF . . .	COLOR/OUTFIT
seraphim	love	red robe or wings
cherubim	knowledge	blue robe or wings
thrones	justice and nature	
dominations	angels	green robe, gold belt
virtues	miracles	green robe, gold belt
powers	demons	green robe, gold belt
principalities	the faithful	golden armor
archangels	the physical world	golden armor
angels	the physical world	golden armor or gown

encounters of the third kind? Maybe the stories of angels (including thrones, see page 34) were told by people who could think of no other way to describe spaceships and aliens than as gods or godlike beings.

	SYMBOL /IDENTIFIER
	swords of fire, six wings
	fire, sapphires, stars
	many eyes
	orb or scepter
	golden staff
	God's seal
	weapons, lilies, streamers
	weapons, lilies, streamers
	weapons, lilies, streamers

AN ALTERNATIVE VIEW: THE TREE OF LIFE

In the Kabbalah (Jewish mystical teaching) there are ten *sefirot*, or angels, that rule channels of divine energy. They stand in a tree, and open like roses. Their names mean Foundation, Splendor, Eternity, Beauty, Power, Grace, Knowledge, Wisdom, Understanding, and Crown. The tree is guarded by the angel Sandalphon, whose height is greater than the diameter of the universe. The tree is topped by Metatron, whose body is flame, whose eyes are unnumbered, and who has seventy-two wings.

What Angels Do

WHAT IS THE PURPOSE OF AN ANGEL?

You know what angels do because you see them doing it in movies, on greeting cards, on stained-glass windows.

They play music, sing, fly around, and watch over people.

They scoop up children who are about to dash into the street, and save them from getting run over by cars.

They whisper into the right ears of people who are about to commit crimes. (Sometimes a demon whispers in the left ear, so that the person gets confused: good? bad? GOOD? BAD!)

Sometimes they might even fight crime, wearing armor and carrying swords, like holy superhero knights with wings.

> **MAJOR MESSAGE: Being holy means being without sin. Angels, by definition, can't sin. To sin, you must have free will, meaning you can choose to go against God's will.**

According to Islam, angels have no free will; they were created to do God's work. Therefore, in Islam, there are no fallen angels.

In other religions, angels can and do rebel against God. Once they do, they are no longer true angels, because they're no longer holy. They are thrown out of heaven, and live in hell as fallen angels.

Angels seem to fly—or

THEY SAW ANGELS

Twentieth century
In 1985 six Russian cosmonauts orbiting Earth in the *Soyuz 7* space station— reportedly all atheists—saw a dazzling orange light that transformed into the figures of seven angels hundreds of feet tall.

fall—somewhere between superheroes, ghosts, and fairies: invisible, helpful, strange, and definitely not human. Yet somehow angels are more serious and important than those other beings. Why? Can fairies whisper in God's ear to change the way things go? Can superheroes whisper in your ear to remind you of an answer on a test? No. But angels have a direct line to God.

MAJOR MESSAGE: People of many faiths and cultures agree that there are such creatures as angels who seem to know more than we know, feel what we feel, and cry with us when we cry. Although they praise God, love God, and work for God, they love us and work for us, too. This is why human beings love angels. Angels represent a better way, a more true goodness than seems possible in this world. And yet, angels also represent our best efforts to be good. Many people consider the ones they love to be their angels. But we also try to be angels to those we love.

A commercial comes on your television: Along with photographs of dogs and cats in animal shelters, a voice tells you that you can be an angel to a pet that needs rescuing. In this situation, you don't need the voice to define the word *angel* for you. You understand that being an angel to a pet means adopting it, feeding it, taking care of it, loving it. Without you, the homeless dogs and cats are helpless, but you can make a miracle in their lives by taking them out of the chaos of the shelter and giving them a warm, happy home. Isn't this what we hope angels—the kind with wings and halos—will do for us?

Then again, some people say their pets are their angels: beings who love us without question and remind us that there is more to life than the daily grind. Yes, we hope angels will do this for us too.

> **MAJOR MESSAGE: All the religions agree: Angels exist because God created them to help with his work. They are God's staff.**

What is God's work? That's an enormous question, one nobody can possibly answer in full. But angels give us a hint. Like any staff, there are some angels that are superior to others. In Chapter Two, you read about the nine ranks of angels, all with different jobs. This

He Saw an Angel

Nineteenth century

After Joseph Smith met the angel Moroni, he founded the Mormon Church. Smith was seventeen the first time he saw Moroni, on September 21, 1823, at home in his room in Palmyra, New York. He saw him again more than twenty times after that. Moroni told Smith where to dig up golden plates studded with Egyptian-style hieroglyphics that Smith was said to have translated into the Book of Mormon.

chapter looks at some of the jobs they do.

There are four main tasks for angels. One task is to praise God continually. The second task is to carry messages from God to us. The third task is to do battle against evil. The fourth category of angel work is more miscellaneous, but all the other tasks angels do add up to doing God's work.

1. Angels give God praise.

It could take the form of chanting, singing, or playing. But there are also some angels who are said to be silent, listening to the praise.

ANGELS IN YOUR LIFE

Whether you've ever seen an angel or not, today's angelologists say you can meet one, and that meeting your angel will help you get what you want from your life.

Angel workshops are held all over the country. Some have religious connections. Others are linked to New Age meditations.

Angel counselors contact angels on behalf of their clients or students for help in healing and life coaching. Some of them use angel cards—decks of cards that feature specific angels and their advice or thoughts.

All this is meant to bring people closer to God as well as to help them find their best selves. People who are involved with these activities are comforted and inspired. *What do you think?*

Are angels musicians? Sure. You probably even know which instruments they play.

The archangel Gabriel will play "the last trumpet" on Judgment Day. The Book of Revelation in the Christian New Testament says that the most important seven angels will sound trumpets at the last moments of the universe. The last trumpet will announce the start of the reign of Jesus Christ.

> *Holy, holy, holy is the Lord of Hosts; the whole earth is full of his glory.* —The Bible: Isaiah 6:3
>
> *Holy, holy, holy is the Lord God Almighty, who was and is and is to come.*
> —The Bible: Revelation 4:8
>
> *Gloria in excelsis deo! (Glory to God in the highest!)* —The beginning of the Doxology, or Angelic Hymn, comes from the words the angels said when Jesus was born

Harps, lutes, lyres, and other stringed instruments are often found in the hands of angels, as are horns and drums. Artists often show angels "making a joyful noise unto the Lord." Music is considered part of the continuous praise for God that is one of the angels' chief responsibilities.

Note: In ancient Greece, winged creatures called harpies (which were like birds with women's heads and breasts) would sing and play their harps to sailors.

Angels sing like—yes, like angels. What do they sing?

The Islamic angel Israfil is the Angel of Music, as well as the Angel of Judgment Day, the day when all souls are sent either to heaven or hell. Israfil's horn is made in honeycomb shapes like beehives; each hexagon holds one of the souls of the dead.

Christian monks and nuns sometimes follow a schedule of worship through song that is said to follow the angels' schedule for singing praise in heaven. Eight times a day they stop to sing. Some orders take vows of silence, which they only break to sing praise to God.

2. Angels carry messages.

The word *angel* comes from the Hebrew word *mal'akh*. (Hebrew is the language used by the writers of the Jewish holy books.) This word once meant "the shadow side of God"—the side away from all that light—

IS THIS AN ANGEL?

Fundraisers are often called angels, especially in the theater. Theater angels are people who provide the money needed to stage a show. But why are they called angels? Because they're (literally) in the wings, helping, pushing the show forward. For directors, actors, and musicians, "angels" can seem to make miracles.

but then came to mean "messenger." When *mal'akh* was translated into Greek, the word *aggelos* was used. In Latin, the language of the Christian Bible, the words used included *nuntius*, which means divine (holy) messenger, and *angelus*, human messenger.

In the Qu'ran, the holy book of Islam, angels are called *malaika*, which means "messengers." As in the other holy books, they intermediate between Allah and the mortal, physical world.

What kind of messages do angels bring?

Angels are go-betweens. They carry messages from God, and take our concerns to God—acting as our representatives in heaven, and God's representatives on Earth. Angels don't usually bring bad news, and they try to calm the people to whom they bring messages.

Angels bring information. They tell us the truth.

Some say it was God Himself who spoke to Moses on Mount Sinai. Some say it was the Angel of the Lord. Who is this Angel of the Lord? Some theologians think it is God Himself, or his son, Jesus Christ, taking the form of an angel.

> *The Lord bless you and keep you. The Lord make his face to shine upon you, and be gracious to you. The Lord lift up his countenance upon you, and give you peace.*
> —The Litany of the Angels, from the Dead Sea Scrolls

MAJOR MESSAGE: *Angels let us know everything is going to be all right. Angels bring us warnings. Angels ask us to help others. Angels show us reasons to love God and other people.*

How do angels talk to people? They talk and write. Emanuel Swedenborg said that angels express love in their vowels and ideas in their consonants. He said that angels never argue or show uncertainty, because their main message is always how much God loves us.

The ancient city of Mahanaim, in what is now Jordan, was named by Jacob, who camped there. Mahanaim means "two camps," referring to Jacob's camp and to the camp of the angels who visited him there. Mahanaim was situated along the Jabbok River in what is now Jordan, across the river from Penuel, where Jacob would go next—and wrestle an angel all night.

Angels speak all languages, but how do angels write?

In Angelic Script or the Alphabet of the Ark, letter and sound forms are derived from Hebrew. There is also writing called Enochian Script, said to have been given to Enoch by the angels. Twenty-first-century angelologists will sometimes suggest that people learn this writing so that they can communicate with their angels.

What do angels write? They write your name in the book of life. The *malaika* of Islam are guardians to mankind. They keep track of everyone's doings in writing at Allah's command, except for when Allah himself does the writing.

ANGELIC ALPHABET

| thes | cheth | zain | vau | he | daleth | gimel | beth | aleph | zade | pe |

ain   sameth   nun   mem   lamed   caph   iod   tau   schin   res   kuff

Angel messages that form the basis of major religions:

- In the Bible an angel (probably Metatron) stops Abraham from killing Isaac.
- In the Bible an angel tells Hagar, a maid who has run away from her master, to leave the wilderness and go back home.
- In the Bible angels gave the Ten Commandments to Moses, or were present when God gave them to Moses.
- In the Zoroastrian holy book the angel Vohu Manah (whose name means "good mind") gave God's message to Zoroaster more than 2,500 years ago.
- In the New Testament the angel Gabriel gave the news of the coming of St. John the Baptist and Jesus to their mothers and announced Jesus's birth to the shepherds.
- In the New Testament, Gabriel stayed with Jesus and supported him as Satan challenged him.
- In the Qu'ran the angel Gabriel dictated the Qu'ran to Muhammed.
- In the Book of Mormon the angel Moroni came to Joseph Smith to bring him the Book of Mormon.

3. Angels do battle against evil.

The archangel Michael is often shown wearing armor

In Heaven an angel is nobody in particular.
—George Bernard Shaw

and striding as though into battle. Michael is the leader of the warrior angels.

Angels fight the good fight. God's angels are described as "armies of heaven." They are warriors. Every day people make choices between acting honorably or behaving badly. You might have seen those shown in cartoons as a person with a good angel (with a halo) on one shoulder and a bad angel (horns, pitchfork) on the other. Each of them whispers in the person's ear and tries to win the person over. That's one idea about angels—that they hang around us in pairs.

But many stories tell of the great battle between good and evil that goes on eternally, not just in people's hearts on Earth, but in the realms of heaven and hell, outside time and space. Angels are the soldiers of heaven, and the devil and his forces (all angels that have turned to the dark side) are the soldiers of hell.

4. *Angels carry out God's work.*

Angels run the world. Angels keep the world working, maintaining the natural order of things. When harmony is disrupted (as in a storm), angels are in charge of that, too. During the Middle Ages, angels were said to be in charge of the laws of nature: It wasn't gravity that kept you from flying off Earth into space, it was angels. They pushed the stars and planets, controlled the sun and moon. In the 1400s, when people

BOOK ANGEL

In Philip Pullman's *His Dark Materials* (*The Golden Compass*, *The Subtle Knife*, and *The Amber Spyglass*), the Authority is the name of the first angel, who was formed of dust. The Authority tells the other angels that he created the universe. Other angels in this series include Metatron, a powerful angel who acts on the behalf of the Authority, and lesser angels, including Baruch and Balthamos, devoted partners who guide the human heroes Will and Lyra. The death of the Authority in *The Amber Spyglass* led many people to ban or condemn Pullman's books.

The word "sinister" literally means "left-handed." This comes from the idea that Satan ruled the left shoulder of every person, trying to lead him or her to the dark side. This is one reason why parents and teachers used to try to "correct" left-handedness by making children write with their right hands.

began to discover the scientific laws behind the forces of motion, gravity, and the movements of the planets, less power was assigned to angels.

Angels help bring about miracles. A miracle is an event that shouldn't happen, scientifically speaking. In a miracle, something physical is overcome through spiritual means—even if you can't tell that this is what's going on. Someone due to die from a fatal disease suddenly recovers. A car is stopped from skidding off a cliff. A starving person finds money in the street. Was it the invisible hand of an angel that made the miracle?

My god has sent his angel and hath shut the lion's mouths, and they have not hurt me.
—The Bible: Daniel 6:22

Angels are there at important moments. Christians and Muslims believe that an angel told Jesus's mother, Mary; Mary Magdalene; and Joanna that Jesus had risen from the dead.

Abou Ben Adhem

Abou Ben Adhem (may his tribe increase!)

Awoke one night from a deep dream of peace,

And saw, within the moonlight in his room,

Making it rich, and like a lily in bloom,

An angel writing in a book of gold:—

Exceeding peace had made Ben Adhem bold,

And to the presence in the room he said,

"What writest thou?"—The vision raised its head,

And with a look made of all sweet accord,

Answered, "The names of those who love the Lord."

"And is mine one?" said Abou. "Nay, not so,"

Replied the angel. Abou spoke more low,

But cheerly still; and said, "I pray thee, then,

Write me as one that loves his fellow men."

The angel wrote, and vanished. The next night

It came again with a great wakening light,

And showed the names whom love of God had blest,

And lo! Ben Adhem's name led all the rest.[4]

—James Leigh Hunt (1784–1859)

A Most Important Angel

Metatron:

- stopped Abraham's hand when he was about to kill Isaac, who would father all of Israel. Some Jewish theologians say that Metatron is the most important angel. In Jewish holy books he is the angel through whom God connects with man.

- is the Heavenly Scribe. Metatron writes everything that happens in the book of life.

- is the biggest angel, eight to thirteen feet tall or, according to the Zohar, as tall as the world is wide.

- is terrifying and fierce with a face more dazzling than the sun. Metatron was probably the angel who led the Israelites through the wilderness.

- is kind and gentle. Some say Metatron is the angel in charge of children who die.

- has seventy-six names, according to the Kabbalah, the mystical teaching of Judaism.

Fallen Angels

WHAT HAPPENS TO BAD ANGELS?

People say they've seen angels. One of the most common moments for sightings seems to be the moment of death. People who have nearly died—and then lived to tell their tales—often report being comforted, guided, or led to "the other side" by beings of tenderness, light, and warmth.

But that's not all. There's another side to the other side. The 1980s movie *Ghost* provided an image that endures in the memory of any who have seen it—and that resonates

About 1500 B.C.
Three angels sat with Abraham under the oaks of Mambre. Abraham didn't know they were angels because they appeared as humans, so he shared his food with them, and they ate. Experts argue about whether these were really angels or God Himself, and whether the immortal angels really ate. The angels tell Abraham that he and his wife will have a son (even though they're very old). The son is Isaac, who will be the father of a great nation—the Jewish people (the nation of Israel). Later, when God tests Abraham, telling him to kill Isaac, an angel stops Abraham from doing it.

with people who have had a different near-death experience. In *Ghost*, when someone good dies, he is enveloped by a white glow, and his face glows with joy. But when someone bad dies, he is attacked by a flapping cloud of bat wings and he is carried away by darkness and horror.

THE ANGEL OF DEATH

What really happens when you die? Your answer may depend on whether you've had a near-death experience, whether you believe the stories of those who have nearly died, or whether your religion or faith teaches you something about life after death.

People of many religions believe in an Angel of Death.

Since angels travel between the physical world and the nonphysical world, it seems natural that they would accompany people as their souls leave their physical bodies and cross over into the nonphysical world. Some believe that guardian angels do this; others think the Angel of Death comes to everyone at his or her time.

• The Midrash (part of the Talmud) says the Angel of Death appeared on the first day that God created the universe, life going hand in hand with death.

• Roman Catholics believe in two Angels of Death: the archangel Michael, who takes people's souls to heaven; and the archfiend Samael, who takes souls to hell.

• In Islam death is a happy moment when humans move closer to heaven. They are guided by Azra'il, the Angel of Death who decides which souls will go back to life in another body, and which will move on toward Allah. Azra'il, who appreciates the connection between people and Paradise, is the angel who brought Allah clay from Earth with which to form Adam.

> ### HE SAW AN ANGEL
>
> *First century*
> *I saw Satan falling like*
> *lightning from heaven.*
> —Jesus, the Bible: Luke 10:18

One version of the Angel of Death that everyone knows—regardless of religion—is the Grim Reaper. You've probably seen pictures of him: He wears a long cloak with a hood over his skull face, and he carries a tall pole with a blade attached to the end. This tool is called a scythe. It is used for cutting down wheat, and symbolizes cutting people out of life.

The Grim Reaper is scary. You don't want to answer a knock on your door and see him there waiting to escort you or someone you love. But, as the "good" deaths in *Ghost* indicate, not all people perceive the moment of death as a scary one. And angels are part of the reason.

The "bad" deaths in *Ghost* represent the fear that many people have of what actually exists on "the other side."

If good exists, does there have to be evil? If so, what form does the evil take? Are there people who are all bad? Are there angels who are evil? And if there is a heaven where only angels can live, is there a hell where only demons can live?

ANGELS OF DARKNESS

According to the Book of Revelation in the Christian New Testament, one third of all angels are fallen. Angels who sin fall into the abyss—layers on layers of hell, with Satan himself at the greatest depth. They battle God's army of angels in a continual war between good and evil. Great artists have depicted the battle between heaven and hell, in which armored angels and demons fight in midair. But some people are sure that the battle really takes

(JUST A FEW) NAMES FOR THE DEVIL

Lucifer	Lord of the Dark Empire
The Beast	Prince of Darkness
Satan	Mephistopheles
Beelzebub (Lord of the Flies)	Old Nick
General of the Diabolic Hordes	The adversary

place within each individual, as our good and bad impulses battle inside us.

> *Abandon all hope, ye who enter here.*
> —Dante, *The Divine Comedy*; these words were written on the gate of hell

The stories of angels of darkness vary widely. Ghost stories, battle stories, myths, fairy tales, scripture, and other religious stories have combined to create our image of the underworld. It includes

BOOK ANGEL

- In Dante's poem *The Divine Comedy*, "The Inferno" tells the story of a journey through Hell, Purgatory, and Heaven. It is a description of the Christian view of the afterlife, and had an enormous effect on people's thoughts about demons, Satan, and angels. Dante Alighieri wrote *The Divine Comedy* between 1308 and 1321, in his home, Florence, Italy.
- In 1673, John Milton, a blind English poet, wrote *Paradise Lost*, an epic poem that chronicled the battle for heaven and hell and told about the lives of the angels in their own voices.
- **Note:** Many of the ideas people today have about angels can be traced back to these two books, and the magnificent illustrations Gustav Doré did for both books. That's why these books get assigned in literature courses in high schools and colleges—because they are a key to how we live and what we believe as a culture.
- In *The Screwtape Letters*, by C. S. Lewis, a father demon councils his son, assigned to a human, on how best to tempt him to sin.

Devils Tower National Monument looks like a landing platform between heaven and earth. The movie *Close Encounters of the Third Kind* made Devils Tower the landing platform for the spaceship of the aliens. But this is not where the name came from. The original names, different for each of the Native American tribes in the area, all included words for "Bear": Bear's House, Bear's Lair, Bear's Lodge, etc. This was because of the gouges along the sides of the rock that look like they were made by a bear's claws. But in 1875 a U.S. government interpreter thought the name meant "Bad God," and named it for the devil.

characters from all kinds of plots, but the story has the same conflict no matter who tells it: kind vs. wicked, good vs. evil, love vs. hate. Details and settings are filled in from the dark, cobwebbed corners of our imaginations.

Hell is described as deep, distant, filthy, fiery, slimy, vermin-infested, smelly, and inescapable. The devil himself has wings like a bat's. He has a tail like a reptile's, and sometimes transforms into a serpent. He has horns, a beard, and hooves like a goat (or like the pagan god Pan, who ruled nature, fertility, and sex). He sweet-talks like the Big Bad Wolf, acts as jealous as the Wicked Witch of the West, sneaks around like a hungry rat, gives as much cruelty and pain as Darth Vader, lies like a deadbeat dad, and hates as much as Voldemort.

Yet most stories say the devil was God's favorite angel. What happened?

THE FALL

Stories about the Fall feature a power struggle between God and the angel who would become the leader of hell. The idea that there is an ongoing, perpetual battle between good and evil came from Zoroaster.

MAJOR MESSAGE: *Some people think that the battle between heaven and hell began when angels grew jealous of man—and that one angel was more jealous than the rest.*

Lucifer was once known as the Morning Star. His name

means "Bringer of Light." Now he's known as "the Prince of Darkness." The being who became Satan used to be "the anointed cherub," perfect and beautiful and given a high position by the grace of God. But Satan became too proud, and challenged God. He was cast out of heaven and sentenced to eternity in the lake of fire. How did this happen?

You might have sympathy for the devil if you've heard this version of his fall: Lucifer was God's brightest angel, the one who loved God most and listened most obediently when God told the angels to bow to none but God himself. And then God created Adam and asked the angels to bow to him. When Lucifer refused, he was cast out of heaven. Now he is condemned to live in hell, where he waits forever in sorrow, hurt, and confusion. He is often called Satan.

In Sunday school classes Christians learn that Adam and Eve were cast out of Eden after

ANGELIC?

Persian *fereshta* are female celestial beings who entertain people who live in Paradise.

Satan, in the form of a serpent, tempted Eve to take a bite of the apple that grew on the Tree of Knowledge. Satan did this because he was jealous of the high position of humans and wanted to bring them down.

He proved that giving man freedom of will was a dangerous part of God's plan, and he was condemned to eternity in hell because of it.

The Book of Revelation, in the New Testament, tells how the archangel Michael and his soldiers went to war against Satan and his evil followers. When Satan fell, angels rained from the sky. When John wrote the Revelation, he stated that a third of God's angels had gone over to the dark side and become the devil's messengers. On Earth, they battle for people's souls.

THERE IS NO DEVIL IN JUDAISM

Jews don't believe in the Devil. There is an angel—or some being—with the name Ha-satan, which means "the

THE NEPHILIM

In Genesis 6, around 2000 B.C., male angels—the "sons of God"—paired up with human women, the "daughters of men." Their children are described as *nephilim*, which means "the fallen." The nephilim were giants, mighty people. Because of them, God decided on a new start: He would send the Great Flood to wipe out every living thing. Noah was chosen to carry on the race of men, which started all over again when the floodwaters dried up. But many stories say that the nephilim were not wiped out after all, and that they became demons.

adversary" or "the opponent," almost like someone who argued with God. But Ha-satan is not seen as God's enemy, and has only a small role in the scriptures in which he appears.

The Old Testament has no reference to fallen angels, and doesn't mention the idea of good or bad angels at all.

THE ZOROASTRIAN DEVIL

In Zoroastrianism, each of the six important archangels—the amesha-spentas—exists at first only to help Ahura Mazda (God), but eventually has an opposing archfiend. The amesha-spentas each govern an aspect of life, or Earth or beyond, and the archfiends battle them for this realm. Zoroastrianism introduced the idea of an ongoing battle between good and evil.

THE CHRISTIAN DEVIL

Christians associate the devil with death. To Christians, the way to conquer death is to follow Jesus. Then, even if someone sins, a place is reserved for him or her in heaven. But even Jesus had to do battle with Satan; God sent Jesus to fight the battle with "the Beast" on the behalf of all people.

> From morn
> To noon he fell, from noon to dewy eve,
> A summer's day; and with the setting sun
> Dropp'd from the zenith like a falling star."
> —John Milton, describing the fall of Lucifer in *Paradise Lost*

THE MUSLIM DEVIL

According to Islam, there are no fallen angels, but there

A MOST IMPORTANT ANGEL

Lucifer:
- has a name that means "shining one" or "star of the morning" (Isaiah 14:12). Other names for Lucifer include Dragon of Dawn and Prince of the Power of Air.
- gives birth to Sin through his head.
- has twelve wings, to set him above all other angels.
- lives now in hell or the underworld, also called the pit or Sheol (according to Jewish scripture).
- **Note**: One Egyptian god, Sata—a serpent God—fell to Earth.

are Jinns (or djinns), led by Iblis, the enemy of mankind. Jinns are spirits made of fire, not light. Unlike angels, they have free will, and can go against God's wishes.

Just as the stories of angels and heaven have many parallels in mythology and folklore, the descriptions of the devil and hell borrow characters and settings—for example, the Underworld of Hades in Greek mythology and the figure of Pluto, the banished, angry god of Roman myths.

WHO'S WHO OF HELL

Archfiend—Satan is the archfiend. Everyone else in hell is a fiend.

Princes of Hell—There are seven of these, parallel to the most important seven angels. According to the Zohar, the most important prince is the Angel of Death.

Devils—This word's roots give it a variety of possible meanings: spirit, god, liar, adversary.

Devils are considered to have once been angels, while demons come from the Nephilim—also called the Watchers,

IS THIS AN ANGEL?

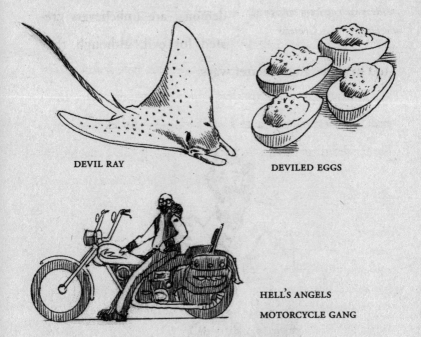

DEVIL RAY

DEVILED EGGS

HELL'S ANGELS
MOTORCYCLE GANG

Sons of God, or Grigori—born when angels paired with human women.

Demons are immortal souls who always choose wrong over right, lies over truth. Some theologists say angels can lead demons back to the right path.

> Better to reign in hell than to serve in heaven.
> —John Milton, *Paradise Lost*

Powers are the angels with the most control over demons.

In Islam, *shaitans*, like demons, are unbelievers created for evil, although they too may be taught better ways.

Some characteristics of the pagan god Pan, god of fertility, nature, and sex, were transferred to Satan by artists from medieval times.

HORNS

WINGS

TAIL

HAIR

DO YOU BELIEVE IN HEAVEN? IN HELL?

"I believe in heaven."[5]

"I believe in hell."[5]

Look!
An Angel!

WOULD YOU KNOW AN ANGEL IF YOU MET ONE?

I f you heard someone described as an angel, you'd know what that meant, wouldn't you?

And if you felt that an angel had been with you, you could explain that feeling, couldn't you?

Sometime, somewhere, human beings got the idea that there were these other beings—strong and beautiful—who could help with the pain and difficulty of life in a world governed by space and time.

Since the beginning of human history, people have believed in beings that were not limited by space and time. These beings have included ghosts, gods and goddesses, fairies, elves, superheroes, extraterrestrials—and yes, angels.

> Be not forgetful to entertain strangers: for thereby some have entertained angels unawares.
> —The Bible: Hebrews 13:1–2

What do angels look like?

They come in two main varieties: beautiful ghosts with long hair and beautiful outfits, who are girly looking even if they're male, showing off their wings, their halos, and their really good behavior.

ANGELIC IDEA

Emanuel Swedenborg, a Swedish angelologist, said that an angel can assume a material body for a moment, so that people can see it. He also said that people can see angels with their spiritual or inner eye, depending on how aware and open-minded the people are—or how much they need an angel.

OR

Fat, naked babies with wings too small to hold them up when they fly, who sometimes are funny and sometimes sneak up on people.

Over their heads, they all have glowing circles called halos.

Some people, people who say they have seen angels with

their own eyes, say angels really have wings and halos.

But angel appearance is a tricky thing, because if angels have to take physical forms to be seen, they may take forms that people will recognize as angels. If an angel wanted to be recognized as an angel, wouldn't he or she put on that kind of outfit, the way you would if you wanted to be an angel for Halloween?

In some Bible stories angels don't appear that way at all. In the Book of Numbers, Balaam's path is blocked by an invisible angel, until God decides to open Balaam's eyes. In some other Old Testament stories angels appear as everyday humans. They aren't described as having wings or halos.

> It seems [angels] take whatever form the visited person is willing to accept, and sometimes no form at all—a dream, a thought, a surge of power, a sense of guidance.
> —Sophy Burnham, *A Book of Angels*

The holy books of the great religions all have stories about angels. People believed these stories were sent by God

TEN ANGEL SONGS
(NOT COUNTING CHRISTMAS CAROLS)

"Heaven Must Be Missing an Angel"	"Teen Angel"
"Angel of the Morning"	"My Angel Baby"
"Angel on My Shoulder"	"I'm No Angel"
"(The Angels Want to Wear My) Red Shoes"	"Your Guardian Angel"
"Earth Angel"	"Lips of an Angel"

to prophets who wrote them. Other stories were told by "witnesses," people who said they had seen angels for themselves. All these stories were passed down and retold over thousands of years, storyteller to listener, mother to child, book author to reader.

The stories had some things in common: The angels

weren't humans. They came from God. They appeared and disappeared, made odd things happen, and carried God's messages. They were superstrong, superknowledgeable, superpowered, supernatural.

MAJOR MESSAGE: Who knows who was the first person to describe angels as having wings or shining with a strange light? One thing is for sure: Most of our ideas about what angels look like come from people who have made images of them—painters and sculptors.

Imagine wanting to paint or sculpt an angel based on a story you've heard about the angel's doings. You'd have to decide what angels looked like. That's an artist's job. And artists who looked for ideas back in the early days of angel stories didn't have to look any farther than the stories that were told about gods and goddesses.

Even before there were stories about angels, there were stories about the Greek goddesses Nike or Iris, the goddess of the rainbow, or the Greek god Hermes. Both of them have wings to carry them quickly between Earth and Mount Olympus, where the gods live.

Then there were the giant guardians carved at the doorways of palaces of ancient Assyria—beings with the bearded heads of men, the bodies of bulls or lions, and beautiful wings. There were even the fossilized bones of dinosaurs to give the idea that once, large beings—some with enormous

ANGELIC?

In Malaysia freckles are called angel kisses.

wings—had walked the Earth. Some people say such finds are where the idea of angels came from, as well as giants—and dragons, too.

As artists sculpted and painted angels, they followed in one another's footsteps, until everyone "knew" what angels looked like: similar to gods and goddesses, ghosts, fairies, birds . . . And today, in the twenty-first century, we have the interesting phenomenon of angels—an understanding not only of what they look like, but what they do.

HE SAW AN ANGEL

560 B.C.
Ezekiel the prophet describes a visit to heaven, where he sees the throne of God, surrounded by seraphim and cherubim, whom he describes as having the faces of oxen. Ezekiel's report is one of the most important sightings of angels. It is specific in detail and even in date: The fifth day of the fourth month of the thirtieth year of the captivity of the Jews in Babylon—about 560 B.C.

Over time, as people have retold the stories of angels and illustrated them, our view of angels has changed to the ones we have today and everyone began to accept these images as pictures of angels. And yet, when you delve deeper into what people know about angels, you realize that there isn't much

She Saw an Angel

Fourteenth century
St. Francesca of Rome said her guardian angel's face was so bright, she could read by its light. St. Francesca said her angel looked like an eight-year-old child.

reason to think angels have gowns, or wings, or halos— or that you could actually see them at all. It's more likely that if angels appeared to people as they really are, people wouldn't be able to stand to look at them. Why? Because they are made of light unless they decide to take a physical form.

Are angels animals? In some stories, angels take the form of animals. In the Bible, in the first book of Kings, the prophet Elijah is fed by two ravens when he is hiding in the desert. Some think the ravens might really be angels.

A Most Important Angel

Raphael:
- is a seraph, the most important kind of angel.
- is one of the seven angels who stand before God in the Revelation in the New Testament.
- is thought to be one of the three angels (with Michael and Gabriel) who visit Abraham.
- shares his feast day, September 29, with Michael and Gabriel.

Certain Native Americans believe in the special powers of birds such as Raven and Eagle.

Are angels extra tall? As described in the Old Testament, they are. People who dug up dinosaur leg bones thought giants once walked the Earth. These bones may have been hollow, like birds' bones, and the fossils might have included wings or indications of wings. Early people didn't have any idea what kind of creatures might have left these skeletons behind.

Angels are also considered to be extra strong, mighty—stronger than people, for sure, and stronger than fallen angels as well.

What are angels made of?

Stories and histories from the major religions and from many cultures indicate that they are made of light. Or fire. All agree that angels are not made of Earthly materials but of heavenly ones. In other words, they are pure energy, energy they send out continually in waves that vibrate all the way from heaven to Earth and, some say, into hell.

St. Thomas Aquinas said they were made up of thoughts, ideas, and feelings.

Although the Qu'ran doesn't talk about the composition of an angel, Islamic tradition says they are made of light and that they have a form humans can't understand or imagine.

Are angels invisible? In some stories angels are invisible. In the Book of Samuel, in the Bible, the sound of wind in the treetops is an angel passing

SCRIPTURE VERSUS TRADITION

The "tradition" in a religion is what people believe, even if the religion doesn't officially support it. Like Judaism and Christianity, Islam is a major religion with scripture—writings that have been written or dictated by God—as well as a tradition formed of stories written or told by other people. Even though they are not holy or sacred, the traditional stories get passed along too, and may even be folded into things written later that are seen as scripture.

by. In the Book of John, in the New Testament, a wrinkle on the surface of water might be an angel, too. So, even if angels don't take on a physical form themselves, they may do something to make a physical change that people can sense.

MAJOR MESSAGE: Here's the key to understanding how angels look: They are not physical. They aren't made of matter, the way we are—atoms, molecules, bones, skin, hair. But because we can't see things that aren't made of matter, angels materialize when they want to be seen.

Are angels born? Do they die? Of course nobody can really know the answer, but *theologians* (experts on religion) have tried to puzzle it out, and in 1870, the Vatican Council, part of the Roman Catholic Church, announced that angels never die, that they are *eternal*. Eternal also means that they exist outside of time.

Here are a few more theories about the lives of angels:

• They are born every day and die every day, only to be reborn (and redie) again the next day.

• People who follow the Kabbalah, a mystical branch of Judaism, believe that whenever someone contemplates God with the greatest possible love—a *mitzvah*—new angels come from God in response.

• In early Indo-European myths, angels could have children, and they sprouted out of their laps like cabbages, five years old when they were born.

• Emanuel Swedenborg, who studied the idea of angels, said they were the spirits of people who once lived.

The Question of Wings

The answer to this is that many angels in paintings and sculptures have wings, but unless someone could take a photo, nobody is really sure. But angels can pass between heaven and Earth, so most people think they have special powers of flight. Except for cherubim and seraphim, none of the angels in the Bible are described as having wings, but Daniel in the Old Testament and John in the Book of Revelation describe their flight.

Scientists studying the relationship between the bodies and wings of birds have concluded that for an angel to be able to fly, it would need a wingspan of 120 feet. But this is based on the idea that an angel would be the size of an adult human, and made of flesh and bone.

So, do angels really fly? Who knows? If they are made of light, then perhaps they move as light does—at the speed of light, that is. Then again, the speed of light is a law

BOOK ANGEL

The Littlest Angel, by Charles Tazewell is a Christmas story. It represents the first look many children have of heaven and the world of angels. It's one of those stories that doesn't have any basis in Scripture, and includes some ideas that don't either: humans becoming angels after they die, angels offering gifts to the baby Jesus, and more.

of physics. If angels live outside the physical world, they're not bound by physical laws, so they may exceed the speed of light as they move between worlds.

The Question of Halos

When artists wanted to portray someone as being holy, they added a halo. Christian art shows haloed saints—people whose human lives gave them a special status and brought them closer to God. But angels are closer to God than the saints, and their halos signify both that they are made of light and that they are eternal: Like the ring of the halo, their lives have no end. People who have seen angels talk about their light or spots of light—not, specifically, a halo.

The Question of Gender

Early stories of angels seemed to borrow from the stories of goddesses, in terms of appearance and abilities. In the Bible, angels were mainly male, but many people think

> Those who believe not in the Hereafter, name the angels with female names.
> —The Qu'ran, 53:27

the archangel Gabriel is female. In Christian artwork the angels looked androgynous—both male and female—with bodies covered in robes; long hair; and no beards.

As for the *putti* (the fat baby angels), they often seem to be little boys—or, like angels, their private parts are covered.

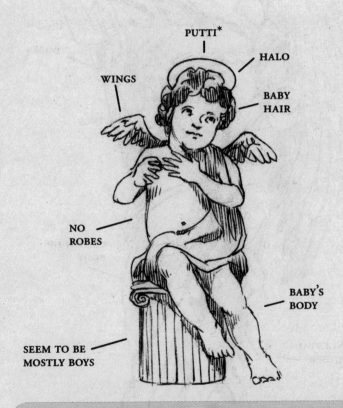

PUTTI*

HALO

WINGS

BABY HAIR

NO ROBES

BABY'S BODY

SEEM TO BE MOSTLY BOYS

*You might hear these little angels described as cherubs. But don't confuse these minor angels with the mighty cherubim (see Chapter Two.)

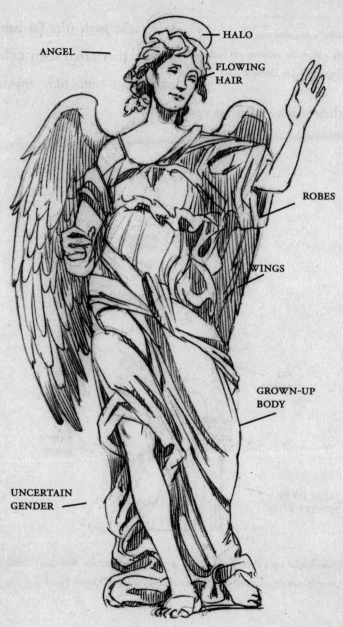

HALO

ANGEL

FLOWING
HAIR

ROBES

WINGS

GROWN-UP
BODY

UNCERTAIN
GENDER

94

Angels in Your Life

HOW CAN YOU CONNECT WITH YOUR ANGEL?

Loads of people say they've seen or talked to angels. In 2006, *Newsweek* reported that 7 percent of Americans said they had felt the presence of a spirit, a dead soul, or an angel.[6]

People have told their angel stories in writing, in interviews with writers, or in angel workshops that have sprouted up around the U.S. in recent years. Workshop leaders report that people telling stories for the first time

THE ANGELUS

When my mother was a girl, the bells of the church in her hometown of Baltimore, Maryland, rang "The Angelus" to remind Catholics to say the prayer of the angels to the Virgin Mary. My mother remembers stopping on the playground to bow her head with her schoolmates and say three Hail Marys. In Europe special bells are rung for The Angelus. They may be inscribed with Mary's name, but many are dedicated to the angel Gabriel.

often tell about something that happened to them years ago. Why haven't they spoken up sooner? Some are afraid other people will think they are crazy. Others are reluctant to share what was a holy, emotional, and sometimes life-changing experience for them. It feels sacred to them; they keep it close to their hearts.

Let's look at some of the things people have reported. *And let's look at the kind of responses they might have gotten.*

• One author of a book on angels was sitting at his desk working on his manuscript when a gorgeous moth hovered over his work. He felt sure that this moth was an angel, and was full of an assurance that he was doing the right thing by writing this book. *Could a moth be an angel? How did the writer get a message from a moth?*

• A couple walking in the woods and mourning the death of their child were visited by two glowing beings with gorgeous wings who talked to them about their grief. It left them with the overwhelming feeling that their child was safe and that all was right with the universe. *Did they really see an angel? Was the sun in their eyes? Were they on drugs? Can angels give people information about their dead loved ones?*

• A high school student whose grades weren't the best was rejected in the first cull by a college's admissions office. Then an admissions officer was asked to read the student essays in the "possibles" file. By mistake she gathered up a folder from the "rejects" file and was convinced by the rejected student's essay to admit him, despite his grades. *Might an angel have guided the admissions officer's hand to the rejected student's file? Or was*

97

this just an accident? Isn't this just an effort to explain a coincidence?

Think back to the description of how angels look, and how most people agree on it. Remember, angels aren't of Earth. They are made of a form of energy that doesn't exist in

ANGELS IN YOUR LIFE

There's a website where you can learn the name of your guardian angel for $1.50. You can download your angel's favorite chant for $1.80 and ask an angelologist a question about angels and receive a personal answer for $1.90. The site promises:

"Among millions of Angels inhabiting the vast Universe at least ONE is monitoring your own mental and spiritual growth since the day of your birth."

When I clicked on the offer to find my guardian angel, the site encouraged me, saying that I would be able to invoke (call on) my guardian angel at the right "frequency" once I knew its name. Frequency is a way that light or sound waves are measured. Angelologists say that angels exist on different planes of light—and that contacting them requires understanding the frequency or vibration where they are found. I was encouraged to pay for the vocalization I would need to call my angel.

He Saw an Angel

our material world. So if angels come to visit, they have to take on a material form that people can see and recognize.

But maybe they don't always do that. Maybe they take on other forms, such as a moth. Even trickier, maybe they can make us do things—sit at a stop sign for a longer time than seems reasonable, check on the baby just one more time, visit someone, or pick up a folder from the wrong pile.

If you think about angel activities this way, then the whole phenomenon of angels gets turned around: What if, instead of imagining an angel acting on your behalf, you find yourself doing something that seems miraculously wonderful for someone else: adopting an old, sick cat when you came to choose a kitten; mailing a letter that's been dropped on the sidewalk; scooping up a toddler who's been knocked over by a wave at the beach?

> **MAJOR MESSAGE:** *Many people give angels credit for the kind of occurrences—what some might call "chance" happenings—that make life surprising and beautiful.*

What would it mean if angels were responsible? We know angels are God's watchers, messengers, guardians. Wouldn't making angels responsible for chance happenings get across the message that God loves us? (And what if the reverse is true—that the devil is responsible for bad things that happen?)

The idea is that we're spiritual beings who are having a human experience here on Earth. This

ANGELIC IDEA

Some angelologists say that your guardian angel mostly stays in the background during your life, coming nearest when you're a child and returning in old age to begin leading you back to the spiritual world.

is what anyone who believes in life after death believes: that life goes on for our souls after our bodies die. In our human bodies, we are separated from the spirit world by being able

to sense only physical things through our eyes, ears, noses, fingers, and mouths. But the same sense of wholeness that allows us to feel the love of our families or anger at injustice also tells us that there might be more to life than the physical world.

Imagine going into a stadium where you knew your mother was waiting to meet you but you didn't know where she was sitting. All you could do is stand there and look for her, knowing she was trying to see you, too. You could probably think of a few ways you could get each other's attention (besides cell phones). Now imagine that someone in a stadium is trying to get your attention and

ANGELIC?

Some angelologists think angels have much in common with the Thunder or Thunderbird gods of the Sioux and other Native Americans.

find you, but you have no idea this person is there. How much slimmer would their chance of getting your attention become?

Maybe it's easier to get messages from God's messengers—angels—if we are aware that somebody might be trying to reach us.

With all the talk in this book about people's beliefs,

A MOST IMPORTANT ANGEL

Gabriel:

- has a name meaning "master of God." Some say he represents the Holy Spirit.
- rules over Paradise.
- (according to Islamic and Christian writings) is the angel who visited the Virgin Mary to tell her that Jesus would be born to her.
- is the patron saint of emergency communications workers (people who respond to 911 calls and dispatch emergency teams). Along with Michael and Raphael, Gabriel's feast day is September 29.
- dictated the Qu'ran to Muhammed. Muslims believe Gabriel gave messages to the prophets to tell them their responsibilities to God. During the holy month of Ramadan, Gabriel visits Earth on Laylat al-Qadr, the Night of Destiny. The angel called Djibril by Muslims has 1,600 wings. On the first Laylat al-Qadr, his wings reached all the way from east to west.
- (according to Mormons) had a human life, as Noah.
- (according to some angelologists) is female.

there hasn't been much said about people who don't believe in God. Why don't they? Maybe their experiences in life have caused them to lose faith. Maybe they feel that God has turned His back on them. Maybe they are furious or sick of God for NOT sending angels to stop the horrible, horrible things that happen on Earth.

The idea that heaven and hell are battling for control over Earth is no comfort to those who are starving, are sick, or have lost their families to war. Where were the angels in the Nazi concentration camps? In the intensive care unit? When the bridge was out and cars drove over the edge? When the tornado came? When the cat got hit by a car? When the college rejection came?

This central mystery of life has no answer. But it does

help explain why people try to hold onto the good things in their lives, and why they believe in angels.

To believe in angels is to believe that God loves you, even as you are full of sorrow. It is to believe that there is goodness in the universe. It is to believe that no matter how dreadful things may seem on Earth, that the score is still two-thirds good angels and one-third bad angels, and that eventually everything will be all right. *What do you think?*

ANGEL THERAPY

Do an Internet search for the word "angel," and you'll find angel therapists. These are people with workshops, books, videos, and websites designed to help customers get in touch with their guardian angels. Some angel therapists may also work as psychics, mediums, or other kinds of spiritual guides. They describe their work as "metaphysics," meaning that what they do transcends the physical world. If angels are the bridge between people and God, then angel therapists may be considered the bridge between people and their angels.

The angel movement is part of the New Age spiritual

movement that began at the end of the twentieth century, a time when people tried new ways to feel stronger inside, more connected to the universe, and more loving toward others. Films like *Pay It Forward* and *Amélie* coincided with ideas like practicing random acts of kindness. They projected the idea that doing kind deeds (even if nobody knew about what you were doing) helped the world and was good for the spirit of the person who did them.

People today—and throughout history—are searching for proof of God's love. They want ways to build stronger relationships with God and to improve their outlook on life.

The statistics don't lie. For more than twenty years now, a strong majority of Americans has said with certainty that they believe in angels. To do so is to believe in God, and to believe in an individual's personal value to God.

> *See that you despise not one of these little ones, for I say to you that their angels in Heaven always see the face of My Father Who is in Heaven.*
> —The Bible, Matthew 18:10
>
> This verse is seen by some Christians as evidence that every person has his or her own guardian angel.

WHO BELIEVES IN GUARDIAN ANGELS?

Jewish Guardian Angels. Many Jews believe that each Jew has eleven thousand guardian angels. Angels are seen as being closely linked to people. Old Testament verses about angels describe how they observe us. In the Psalms, King David writes that God has assigned angels to those who trust in the Lord.

Zoroastrian Guardian Angels. Zoroastrians believe in farohars, guardian angels or spirits who watch over the souls of the living and the dead.

ANGEL PLACES:

At 3,212 feet, Angel Falls, in Venezuela, is the highest waterfall in the world, and 80 percent of that drop is freefall. Despite this, the falls are not named for angels but for a pilot named Jimmie Angel, an American who "found" the remote falls during a flight in the 1930s.

Christian Guardian Angels. Catholics believe that each person has an individual guardian angel, as supported by scripture.

John Calvin (1509–1564) was a Protestant theologian who questioned many Catholic ideas, and provided answers that changed Christianity. He found that Scripture supported the idea that God sent angels to guard people, but not the idea that each person had an individual guardian angel.

> *For if the fact that all the heavenly host are keeping watch for his safety will not satisfy a man, I do not see what benefit he could derive from knowing that one angel has been given to him as his especial guardian.*
> —John Calvin, *Institutes of the Christian Religion*

Islamic Guardian Angels. The *malaika* (messengers) of Islam are guardians to mankind. This allows them to keep an eye on everybody, in order to keep the written records of what each person on Earth does.

Islamic lore says that each person has four Hafazas, a kind of guardian angel: two to watch through the day, and two through the night. They keep track of the good and bad things each person does, recording them in the book of life.

FINDING YOUR ANGEL ON EARTH

One clue to the understanding of people's belief in angels seems to be the *people* or *animals* in their lives that they describe as their angels. Whether your angel on Earth is your mother, your puppy, your teacher, your best friend, your baby brother, your grandfather, the dolphin or celebrity in the poster on your bedroom wall, or the school crossing guard who always tells you to have a good day, you can take a look at that person (or animal) and think about why this is your angel. Does he, she, or it protect you? Love you no matter what you do? Inspire you to be your best? Forgive you if you act like a jerk? Make you feel protective? Make you feel that there is something better, dearer, higher, more important than everyday life? Have a message for you about your life?

Think closely about that last question. It's very important. The person or animal who reminds you that there is something else to be thinking about besides daily life— some goal to push for or something to remember as you go through your day—is likely to be your Earth angel.

But what about those heavenly angels? Angel therapist Doreen Virtue says they are there, two per person, and can be accessed by becoming increasingly aware of the clues and messages they are always trying to give you. Just being aware that your angels are there is the first step, Virtue says. Suddenly when you get an idea to do something, as you decide whether to act on the idea or not, you'll consider where—who—the idea came from. And you'll begin to

IS IT A GHOST, AN ANGEL, OR A FAIRY?

GHOST
spirit of a dead person
caught between heaven and Earth
takes the form it did when alive
misty white, hazy edges
scares us
leaves a chill behind them
is associated with the dark

ANGEL
never lived as a mortal
lives in heaven, may visit Earth
takes different forms
wings, halo
calms us
leaves warmth behind them
is associated with the light

FAIRY
not mortal
lives on Earth
has its own unique form
wings, a soft glow
may help or curse us
our reaction depends on our interaction with the fairy
is neither dark nor light

recognize the guiding hands that are trying to move you onto paths that are right for you.

Plenty of people are skeptical about the existence of angels. Maybe a guardian angel is just a personification of our conscience, that small voice in the back of our heads that tries to keep us from doing the wrong thing. Maybe it is this conscience that protects us, not some spirit.

What do you think? Do you believe that you have a guardian angel, a specific spiritual angel who watches you, influences you, and protects you? Can you see why people would *want* to believe this? Having a guardian angel means that God cares for you specifically, that through this angel you're in touch with God.

Here's a fact, coming now at the end of this book in which I have had to be very careful about stating things as fact:

The only way you'll know whether you have angels in your life or not is to look into your own heart and do your own study of things. Some people feel the presence of angels strongly; others do not. Maybe they are there— or not there—whether or not you're aware of them. Maybe you can have a happy life with or without acknowledging them. Maybe you can have a happy life whether they are there or not. These are questions that don't have answers that can be found in a book. Maybe, with angels, asking the questions is the important thing. *What do you think?*

Glossary

ANGEL—immortal being that intercedes between God and man; an angel of the rank ninth closest to God, and closest to humanity

APOCRYPHA—writings that are not scripture (written or dictated by God) but are part of religious traditions

ARCHANGEL—one of the most important angels (there are between four and seven); an angel of the rank eighth closest to God

CHERUB (plural: cherubim)—an angel of the rank second closest to God

DEMON—a spirit or soul on the path of evil

DEVIL—the leader of the fallen angels

DOMINATION, DOMINION—an angel of the rank fourth closest to God

EARTH—the realm of mortals

ETERNAL—undying, existing outside time and space

HALO—a disk or circle of light used in art to show

holiness; some witnesses report seeing halos over the heads of holy beings such as angels

HEAVEN—the realm of God and angels

HELL—the realm of the devil and fallen angels

HIERARCHY—a system of rankings that shows who stands where

POWER—an angel of the rank sixth closest to God

PRINCE, PRINCIPALITY—an angel of the rank seventh closest to God

SCRIPTURE—writings by God, directed by God (through an angel), or dictated by God (through a prophet)

SERAPH (plural: seraphim)—an angel of the rank closest to God

THEOLOGIAN—someone who studies God and religion

THRONE—an angel of the rank third closest to God

VIRTUE—an angel of the rank fifth closest to God

Bibliography

BOOKS

- Abadie, M. J. *The Everything Angels Book: Discover the Guardians, Messengers, and Heavenly Companions in Your Life.* Avon, Massachusetts: Adams Media, 2000.
- Anderson, Joan Wester. *An Angel to Watch Over Me: True Stories of Children's Encounters with Angels.* New York: Ballantine, 1994.
- Burnham, Sophy. *A Book of Angels.* New York: Ballantine, 1990.
- Davidson, Gustav. *A Dictionary of Angels.* New York: Free Press, 1967.
- Godwin, Malcolm. *Angels, An Endangered Species.* New York: Simon & Schuster, 1990.
- Guiley, Rosemary Ellen. *The Encyclopedia of Angels.* New York: Checkmark/Facts on File, 2004.
- Rochberg, Francesca. *The Heavenly Writing.* Cambridge: Cambridge University Press, 2004.
- Virtue, Doreen. *Divine Guidance: How to Have a Dialogue with God and Your Guardian Angels.* Los Angeles: Renaissance, 1998.
- Walker, Barbara G. *The Woman's Encyclopedia of Myths and Secrets.* New York: HarperCollins, 1998.

BOOKS REFERRED TO IN BOOK ANGELS SECTION

- Alighieri, Dante. *The Divine Comedy*, written 1308–1321, Italy.
- Almond, David. *Skellig.* New York: Delacorte, 1999.

- Gaiman, Neil, Sam Kieth, Mike Dringenberg, et al. The Sandman series beginning with Vol. 1: *Preludes and Nocturnes*. New York: Vertigo, 1993.
- L'Engle, Madeleine. *A Wind in the Door*. New York: Square Fish, 1973.
- Lewis, C. S. *The Screwtape Letters*. New York: HarperCollins, 2001. Originally 1942.
- Milton, John. "Paradise Lost," written 1673, England.
- Pullman, Philip, *His Dark Materials* series, which includes:
  The Golden Compass. New York: Alfred A. Knopf, 1995.
  The Subtle Knife. New York: Knopf, 1997.
  The Amber Spyglass. New York: Knopf, 2000.
- Tazewell, Charles. *The Littlest Angel*. Nashville: Ideals Children's Press, 2001. Originally 1946.

PLAYS, MOVIES, AND TELEVISION REFERRED TO IN "THEATER ANGELS" SECTION

Plays
- Kushner, Tony. *Angels in America: A Gay Fantasia on National Themes*
- von Goethe, Johann Wolfgang. *Faust*. Germany, 1806.

Movies
- *Angels in the Outfield*, directed by Clarence Brown (1951, Metro-Goldwyn-Mayer).
- *Angels in the Outfield*, directed by William Dear (1994, Buena Vista Pictures).
- *It's a Wonderful Life*, directed by Frank Capra (1946, RKO Radio Pictures).

Television
- "Touched by an Angel," CBS Productions (1994–2003).

Notes

FOREWORD

[1] Gallup News Service. "Americans More Likely to Believe in God Than the Devil, Heaven More Than Hell." June 13, 2007 report describing a poll conducted May 10–13, 2007.

CHAPTER 1

[2] The sources for this chapter's religious and nonreligious groups are adherents.com; for Judaism: jewfaw.com, simpletoremember.com, smh.com; for Islam: islamicpopulation.com, wiki.answers.com, wikipedia.com, factbook.net; for Christianity: wiki.answers.com.

CHAPTER 2

[3] Gustav Davidson, *A Dictionary of Angels.* New York: Free Press; 1967.

CHAPTER 3

[4] James Leigh Hunt. "Abou Ben Adhem." Samuel Carter Hall, ed. *The Book of Gems. The Poets and Artists of Great Britain.* London: Saunders and Otley, 1838.

CHAPTER 4

[5] Gallup News Service. "Americans More Likely to Believe in God Than the Devil, Heaven More Than Hell." June 13, 2007 report describing a poll conducted May 10–13, 2007.

CHAPTER 6

[6] *Newsweek*, "Belief Watch: Dead Zone." October 16, 2006.

If you like horses, you'll love these books:

You and Your Horse

Misty of Chincoteague

King of the Wind

Justin Morgan Had a Horse

Take the Reins

Chasing Blue

Behind the Bit

Triple Fault

Best Enemies

Little White Lies

Rival Revenge

Home Sweet Drama

FROM ALADDIN
PUBLISHED BY SIMON & SCHUSTER

CHECK OUT SOME OTHER GHOSTLY BOOKS FROM ALADDIN:

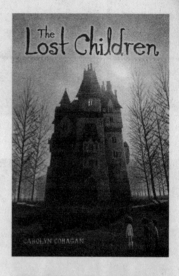

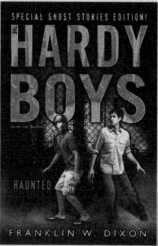

From Aladdin
Published by Simon & Schuster